HAL•LEONARD
INSTRUMENTAL
PLAY-ALONG

CLARINET

COLDPLAY

T0055910

THE CD IS PLAYABLE ON ANY CD PLAYER, AND IS ALSO ENHANCED SO MAC AND PC USERS
CAN ADJUST THE RECORDING TO ANY TEMPO WITHOUT CHANGING THE PITCH!

Cover photo: Peter Neill – ShootTheSound.com

ISBN: 978-1-4768-1832-0

HAL•LEONARD®
CORPORATION

7777 W. BLUEMOUND RD. P.O. BOX 13819 MILWAUKEE, WI 53213

Visit Hal Leonard Online at
www.halleonard.com

CONTENTS

CLOCKS

CLARINET

Words and Music by GUY BERRYMAN,
JON BUCKLAND, WILL CHAMPION
and CHRIS MARTIN

IN MY PLACE

CLARINET

Words and Music by GUY BERRYMAN,
JON BUCKLAND, WILL CHAMPION
and CHRIS MARTIN

EVERY TEARDROP IS A WATERFALL

CLARINET

Words and Music by GUY BERRYMAN,
JON BUCKLAND, WILL CHAMPION, CHRIS MARTIN,
PETER ALLEN, ADRIENNE ANDERSON and BRIAN ENO

FIX YOU

7/8

CLARINET

Words and Music by GUY BERRYMAN,
JON BUCKLAND, WILL CHAMPION
and CHRIS MARTIN

LOST!

9/10

CLARINET

Words and Music by GUY BERRYMAN,
JON BUCKLAND, WILL CHAMPION
and CHRIS MARTIN

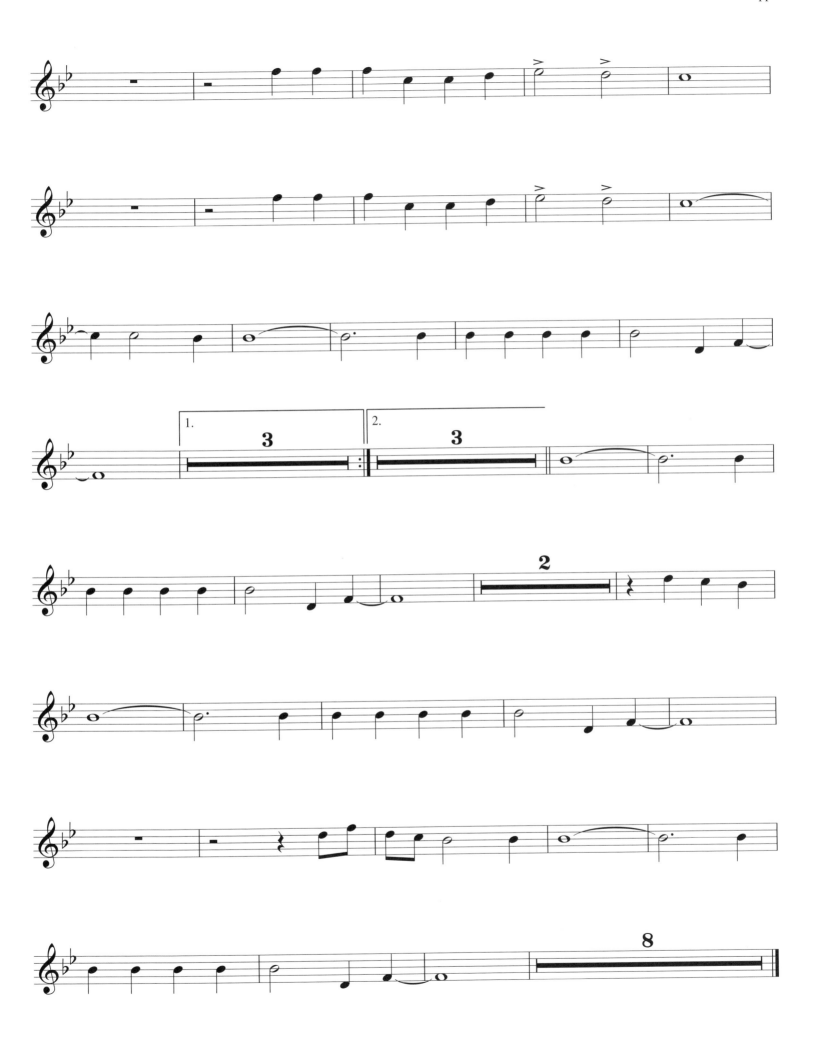

PARADISE

CLARINET

Words and Music by GUY BERRYMAN,
JON BUCKLAND, WILL CHAMPION,
CHRIS MARTIN and BRIAN ENO

THE SCIENTIST

CLARINET

Words and Music by GUY BERRYMAN,
JON BUCKLAND, WILL CHAMPION
and CHRIS MARTIN

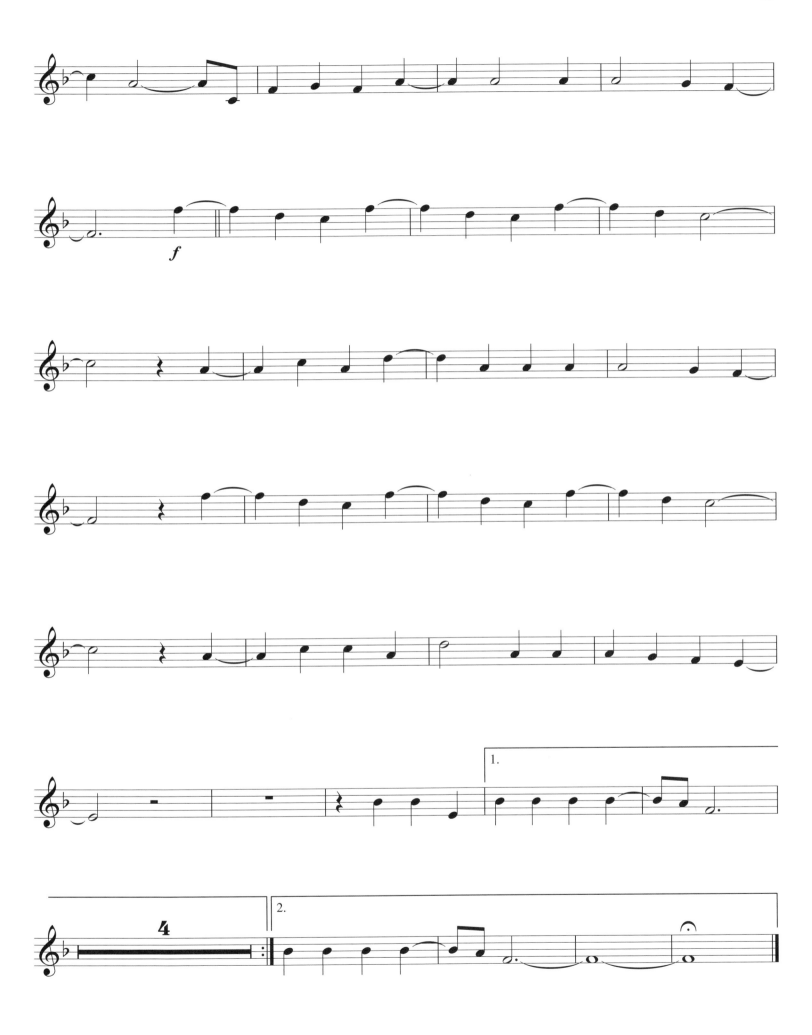

SPEED OF SOUND

CLARINET

Words and Music by GUY BERRYMAN,
JON BUCKLAND, WILL CHAMPION
and CHRIS MARTIN

TROUBLE

CLARINET

Words and Music by GUY BERRYMAN,
JON BUCKLAND, WILL CHAMPION
and CHRIS MARTIN

VIOLET HILL

CLARINET

Words and Music by GUY BERRYMAN,
JON BUCKLAND, WILL CHAMPION
and CHRIS MARTIN

YELLOW

21/22

CLARINET

Words and Music by GUY BERRYMAN,
JON BUCKLAND, WILL CHAMPION
and CHRIS MARTIN

VIVA LA VIDA

CLARINET

Words and Music by GUY BERRYMAN,
JON BUCKLAND, WILL CHAMPION
and CHRIS MARTIN